DEION
SANDERS

DEION SANDERS

Prime Time Player

Stew Thornley

Lerner Publications Company ■ Minneapolis

To Brenda

This book is available in two editions:
Library binding by Lerner Publications Company
Soft cover by First Avenue Editions
241 First Avenue North, Minneapolis, Minnesota 55401

LIBRARY OF CONGRESS CATALOGING-IN-PUBLICATION DATA

Thornley, Stew.
  Deion Sanders : prime time player / by Stew Thornley
     p.   cm. — (The Achievers)
  Summary: Presents the life, from childhood to adulthood,
of one of today's dual sports professionals.
  ISBN 0-8225-0523-1 (lib. bdg.)
  ISBN 0-8225-9648-2 (pbk.)
  1. Sanders, Deion—Juvenile literature. 2. Baseball players
—United States—Biography—Juvenile literature. 3. Foot-
ball players—United States—Biography—Juvenile literature.
[1. Sanders, Deion. 2. Baseball players. 3. Football players.
4. Afro-Americans—Biography.] I. Title. II. Series.
GV865.S22D45   1993
796.357'092—dc20
[B]   92-45686
                                                                          CIP
                                                                           AC

Manufactured in the United States of America

International Standard Book Number: 0-8225-0523-1 (lib. bdg.)
International Standard Book Number: 0-8225-9648-2 (pbk.)
Library of Congress Catalog Card Number:

          1   2   3   4   5   6   98   97   96   95   94   93

Contents

1
Pulling a Deion

Deion Sanders strolled from the on-deck circle toward home plate and glanced at the runner on first base. His team, the New York Yankees, led the Seattle Mariners by five runs. Before stepping into the batter's box, Deion used his bat to draw a half circle in the dirt. He then added a pair of short lines through the half circle. "I've been doing it ever since Little League," he once explained. "I'm not even sure what the shape is."

Finally ready at the plate, Deion sent a Jerry Reed pitch over the right-field fence for a home run. The Yankees led 7-0.

Five days later, dressed in full football gear, Deion Sanders stood near his own 30-yard line. The Los Angeles Rams were about to punt the ball to him. Deion had already returned one punt that day for 15 yards on his first play as a member of the Atlanta Falcons.

He began waving his arms toward the stands, trying to pump up the Atlanta fans. The ball was kicked, and Deion stood under it. He momentarily bobbled the ball, then quickly gained control of it and took off to his right. He was hit by two would-be tacklers on the 32-yard line, changed direction, and circled all the way to his own 20 before heading back upfield.

He was hit three more times, but spun away each time and broke into the open field. He waved to the last defender and high-stepped toward the end zone, capping off a 68-yard punt return. With the touchdown and the extra point that followed, another Deion Sanders team enjoyed a 7-0 lead.

This first ever combination of two such events in the same week—a major-league home run and a National Football League touchdown by the same athlete—occurred in September 1989.

In the past, it was not unheard of for an athlete to compete in different sports in the same year. The seasons of various sports, however, got longer and their schedules began to overlap. The two-sport athlete, forced to make choices, became a rarity.

This changed in 1987 when Bo Jackson, a Kansas City Royals outfielder, announced he would play football for the Los Angeles Raiders after the baseball season ended.

Although his participation in professional baseball and football followed Bo's, Deion has forged his own

Deion combines brashness
with ability on the field.

reputation as a two-sport athlete. His determination
has carried him to new professional athletic heights,
even to the point of being ready and available to play
both sports on the same day.

Deion makes his mark off the field, as well as on.
His flashy clothes and brash confidence have earned
him the nicknames "Prime Time" and "Neon Deion."
Deion defends his image, saying, "If you look good,
you feel good; you feel good, you play good; you play
good, they pay good."

Comparisons to Bo Jackson are inevitable. Even
Deion's agent once called him "Bo Jackson with a

Comparisons to Bo Jackson
are inevitable.

personality." And Bo's comments regarding Deion
have not always been complimentary. Bo has suggested that Deion should do his talking with his
athletic accomplishments rather than with his mouth.
Deion responded to the criticism by saying, "I think
he's just jealous that somebody else is trying to do
what he's doing."

Deion has tried to end the comparison. When he
was playing for the New York Yankees in 1989 and
also thinking about going to work for the Atlanta
Falcons, reporters asked if Deion would be "pulling a
Bo" by playing two sports. "No," he replied, "I'd be
pulling a Deion."

2
Off Anderson Avenue

Most of the people who live in the neighborhood surrounding old Anderson Avenue in Fort Myers, Florida, are poor. Drug dealers roam the streets, preying on young people.

Deion Sanders grew up just off Anderson Avenue. Although the street has since been renamed Martin Luther King Boulevard, the neighborhood remains much the same as it was when Deion lived there.

Those who knew him when he was a young man say two things helped Deion steer clear of the drug dealers: sports and his mother, Connie.

Deion's parents were divorced when he was very young. About five years later, his mother married a man named Willie Knight. To help keep Deion off the streets, Connie Knight allowed her son to play all the sports he wanted. "The streets will raise you or your parents will raise you," one of Deion's coaches later said. "She raised him."

Deion was playing T-Ball (a form of baseball in which the ball is not pitched, but is hit off a tee) at the age of five. Lee Memorial Hospital—where Deion was born on August 9, 1967—overlooked the field on which he played. His mother worked at the hospital and could watch her son as he played. Later, Connie worked at the refreshment stand at the field where Deion played Little League baseball.

Deion loved to show off his great speed on the baseball diamond. He often tried to steal home when the catcher threw the ball back to the pitcher. Even when the steal attempt failed, Deion generated excitement. Once, when trying to steal home in a Little League game, he was trapped off third base in a rundown. He darted up and down the baseline about ten times while the opposing infielders threw the ball back and forth, trying to tag him out. He somehow managed to make it safely back to third base. The fans gave the team in the field a standing ovation just for denying him another steal of home.

Deion was attracted to all sports. In 1977 he began playing on the Fort Myers Rebels, a Pop Warner youth league football team. In his three years on the squad, the team won 38 games and lost only one. The Rebels won the national Pop Warner Championship in 1979 with the help of Deion's three touchdowns. Rebels coach Dave Capel estimated that Deion scored 120 touchdowns during his career as a Rebel.

In addition to playing either running back or quarterback on offense, Deion played defensive safety. "He loved intercepting passes and loved knocking people down," said Coach Capel. "He could get some revenge for all the times he had gotten knocked down on offense."

Deion transferred from Fort Myers High School to North Fort Myers High School just before his sophomore year. Ron Hoover, the North Fort Myers football

Deion and Rebels coach Dave Capel

coach, had not seen Deion play, so he didn't know what the 130-pound newcomer could do. As a result, Deion played very little his first year at his new school.

Deion grew during the following year, and from then on he spent little time on the sidelines. Deion played quarterback on offense and safety on defense. "He was a great safety," said Hoover. "The other teams didn't throw many passes in the middle of the field with Deion there. He'd pick them off."

On the other side of the line, Deion was the team's starting quarterback. Midway through his senior year, Deion was even allowed to call his own plays —the only quarterback Coach Hoover had ever allowed to do so. Deion could both run and throw. His senior year, he racked up 839 yards passing and 499 yards rushing.

At North Fort Myers, Deion played three sports— football in the fall, basketball in the winter, and baseball in the spring. In his senior year, he was named High School Athlete of the Year by the *Fort Myers News-Press*. He was also named to Southwest Florida all-star teams in all three sports.

Deion thrilled fans in all the sports he played. It was through basketball, though, that he received his famous nickname. A high school teammate, Richard Fain (who also went on to play in the NFL), named Deion Prime Time after he scored 30 points in a game, many of them on dazzling dunk shots.

Deion scored 120 touchdowns as a Rebel in the Pop Warner Football League in the late 1970s.

3
Florida State

The Kansas City Royals drafted Deion after he graduated from high school in 1985 and tried to sign him to a professional baseball contract. The Royals were already familiar with Deion. He frequently stopped by their spring training facility, which was within walking distance of his home in Fort Myers. But Deion had also been offered athletic scholarships from a number of colleges in Florida and surrounding states.

The most attractive of these offers came from Florida State University in Tallahassee. The Florida State Seminoles, the football team coached by Bobby Bowden, needed help on defense. Bowden would give Deion the opportunity to play right away.

Deion decided to go to Florida State, where he could play cornerback, another position in the defensive backfield. Also, his mother had wanted him to attend a college within the state so she could go to his games. Tallahassee is located in the northern part of the state, more than 350 miles from Fort Myers. Even so, Connie Knight never missed a single home game during Deion's four years at Florida State.

More often than not, Deion's impressive speed allowed him to keep opposing receivers from catching passes in his territory. In addition, he could help his teammates by tackling receivers they were trying to cover. He often prevented touchdowns by running all the way across the field to catch receivers who had slipped by other defenders.

Deion played in all but one of Florida State's games in 1985, his freshman year, and only missed that one because of a broken wrist. Deion was in the starting lineup for three of those games, including a 76-14 win over the University of Tulsa. In that game, Deion intercepted a pass and returned it 100 yards for a touchdown.

During that first year, Deion also added punt returning to his arsenal of football talents. In the Tulsa game, he returned five punts for a total of 86 yards. His long runbacks helped set up two Florida State touchdowns.

Playing with a rubber cast to protect his broken wrist in the team's final regular-season game against the University of Florida, Deion ran back a punt 58 yards for a touchdown.

The Seminoles played in the Gator Bowl following the season, beating Oklahoma State. Deion made six tackles and intercepted a pass.

He continued the double duty as both a defensive back and a punt returner in his remaining years at Florida State. The Seminoles usually concentrated on trying to block the opposing team's punt, which left Deion with no one to block for him on the runback. Even so, he became the nation's top punt returner his senior year, averaging 15.2 yards per return. By the time he left school, he held Seminole records for punt returning both for a single season and for a career.

Deion also played baseball at Florida State. He was hampered by an ankle injury his first year, but played a full season as a sophomore in 1987. With the help of Deion, who hit .273 in the College World Series, the Seminoles finished fifth in the nation that year.

During the course of the baseball season, Deion found a way to fit in yet another sport. The Metro Conference Championships in both baseball and track were being held at the same time in Columbia, South Carolina. Deion had asked his baseball coach for permission to participate in the track meet after the end of the baseball game.

After playing right field in a win over Southern Mississippi, Deion jogged over to the track a few hundred yards away. He received a quick lesson in

In addition to playing football, Deion participated in track and played baseball while at Florida State University.

handing off a baton, then ran a leg in the 400-meter relay. Deion helped the Seminoles finish second in the relay, which gave the track team enough points to capture their tenth straight conference championship.

Deion then hustled back to the baseball diamond, where he helped Florida State win the conference championship in baseball by driving in the winning run to beat Cincinnati in his second baseball game of the day.

Deion enjoyed his brief fling on the track so much that he skipped baseball in his junior year to be a full-time member of the track team. In only his third competitive race at 100 meters, Deion turned in a time of 10.26 seconds. The time was good enough to qualify him for both the U.S. Olympic trials and the National Collegiate Athletic Association (NCAA) championships. He was also named Most Valuable Performer of the Metro Conference Championships in 1988 after he won the 100 meters, 200 meters, and ran on the winning 400-meter relay team during the competition.

Football, however, remained Deion's priority. He took part in the NCAA track meet in June that year, but passed up an opportunity to compete in the Olympic trials. The Olympics would not be held until September. If Deion did qualify for the Olympic team, he would miss the first four Florida State football games.

In addition, Deion had plans for his summer other than training for the Olympics. He would be playing professional baseball! Even though he hadn't played baseball at Florida State that year, the New York Yankees selected him in the amateur baseball draft and signed him to a minor-league contract.

Signing a professional contract meant Deion could no longer play baseball in college. He would still be eligible to compete in other sports though. He played six weeks for Yankee minor-league teams, then

Shown here carrying the ball, Deion played both as a defensive back and on special teams in college.

returned to Tallahassee in early August for football practice. Deion wanted to be ready for the Seminoles' season opener against the Miami Hurricanes.

Miami had beaten Florida State by one point, 26-25, in the previous season and had gone on to capture the national championship. The Seminoles finished the year as the number-two team in the country.

Deion hoped his team could avenge that loss in the first game of 1988. Miami won again, however, this time by a score of 31-0. For the second year in a row, the Hurricanes provided Florida State with its only loss. The Seminoles finished the 1988 regular season with a record of 10-1 and earned a spot in the Sugar Bowl in New Orleans.

Deion was gaining national recognition for his work on defense as well as on punt returns. He was also earning a reputation for his "trash talk," as he often hurled insults at opponents and taunted them during games.

"My game has never been quiet," Deion said in response to criticism of his on-field antics. "I get emotional. I take charge of things. That's where the talk comes in."

While Deion's mouth and flashy style sometimes infuriated both opposing players and fans, his attitude also served to fire up his own teammates.

In a game at Clemson University his senior year, the Seminoles trailed 14-7 in the second half. As Deion prepared for a punt return, he turned toward the Clemson bench and hollered, "This one's going back!"

A few seconds later, he returned the punt 78 yards for a touchdown. Crossing the goal line, he struck a pose for the fans in the end zone and yelled, "How you like me now?" The runback sparked a rally that helped the Seminoles win the game.

Deion's last college football game was against Auburn University in the Sugar Bowl in January 1989. During the week before the game, Deion said publicly that he envisioned himself intercepting a last-minute pass to preserve a victory.

In the final minute of the game itself, Florida State clung to a 13-7 lead as Auburn drove down the field. With five seconds left, Deion jumped in front of an

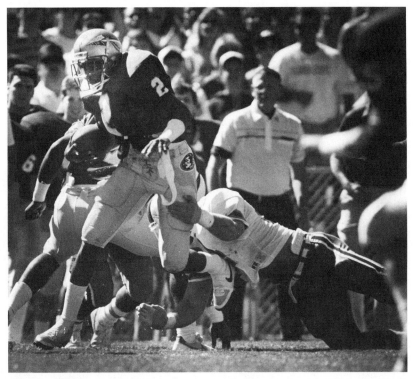

In his senior year, Deion (shown here wearing No. 2) was voted the best college defensive back in the country.

Auburn receiver at the goal line to intercept a pass. His dream became reality. Thanks to Deion's heroics, the Seminoles won the game and ended the season ranked as the number-three team in the nation.

Deion had nearly done it all at Florida State. Two more accomplishments, however, eluded him. One was to win a national football championship. The other was a chance to play basketball for the Seminoles.

Although the timing of the football and baseball seasons prevented him from trying out for the basketball team, Deion did offer to play in a game. "I told Coach [Pat] Kennedy that if they let me play in one basketball game before the fans, I'd be there to stay," said Deion. "I'm a real crowd pleaser."

Kennedy never took him up on the offer, but Deion did receive many honors for the sports he did play. In football, he was an All-American at cornerback in both his junior and senior years. In his senior year, Deion received the Jim Thorpe award, presented annually to the best defensive back in the country.

In Deion's four years at Florida State, the Seminoles had a regular-season record of 34 wins, 9 losses, and 1 tie. They had also played, and won, bowl games following each season.

Prime Time was ready for the pros.

4
Double Duty

"You sprinkle a crowd around me and that's what I like. Then, you'll see what I can do," said Deion Sanders as he prepared to play in his first major-league baseball game.

Deion had played for less than a year in the minors and before much smaller crowds than would be in New York's Yankee Stadium for his May 1989 debut in the big leagues.

An injury to Roberto Kelly had left the Yankees in need of help in the outfield. The Yankees also hoped that promoting Deion to the major leagues might persuade him to make baseball his top priority. A few weeks earlier, Deion had been drafted by the Atlanta Falcons of the National Football League. The Falcons hoped he would be playing for them in the fall.

Deion wasted no time in bringing Yankee fans to their feet. In the top of the first inning, he made a strong throw from center field to cut down a Seattle runner trying to go from first base to third on a single. In the fourth inning, Deion drove in a run. Then, with his team down by three runs, Deion led off the seventh with a single. He started a five-run rally, helping the Yankees to a come-from-behind victory.

Deion's stay with the Yankees was brief. He hit .212 with one home run and used his speed to make some spectacular catches in center field. But when Kelly recovered from his injury and returned to the lineup in mid-June, Deion was sent back to the minors.

Later in the season, the Yankees again called up Deion. He wasn't with the team for long this time either. But this time, the choice to leave was Deion's. During a game in Seattle (the day after Deion's home run off Jerry Reed), he received word that his agent had reached an agreement on a contract with the Atlanta Falcons. After batting in the sixth inning, Deion shook hands with manager Bucky Dent, then left the stadium in order to catch a flight to Atlanta and join the Falcons.

Deion's contract with the Falcons would pay him more than $4 million over four years. It would also allow him to play baseball when he wasn't required to be with the Falcons.

Bo Jackson had made baseball his number-one sport, saying football was his "hobby." Deion's priorities, however, were the other way around. "I'm married to football," he often said. "Baseball is my girlfriend."

But juggling careers in different sports would not be easy. Other athletes use the off-season to rest and to give minor injuries a chance to heal. Deion, however, got little time off between the end of the football season and the beginning of spring training for baseball. Also, his commitment to football meant he would have to leave his baseball team before its season ended.

Although released by the Yankees in 1990, Deion quickly resumed his two-sport status when he was signed as a free agent by the Atlanta Braves early in 1991. But leaving the baseball diamond for the football field was harder for him that year because the Braves were fighting for the pennant. They lost not only Deion during their stretch run, but also outfielder Otis Nixon, who had been suspended for violating the league's drug abuse policy.

Trailing the Los Angeles Dodgers in the standings with 12 games left, the Braves needed help. They asked Deion if he could be available to play for them following Falcon practices and on his days off. Deion agreed.

He played football on Sunday, September 22, and showed up ready for baseball on Tuesday. But the Braves' game with Cincinnati was rained out. The teams would play a doubleheader starting at 4:05 p.m. the next day. Deion had to practice with the Falcons but promised he would show up at the baseball stadium as soon as possible.

Deion had no shortage of offers for rides for the 33-mile trip between the Falcons' practice facility in Suwanee, Georgia, and Atlanta-Fulton County Stadium. But a local television station made the best offer.

At 4:15 p.m., Deion hopped into the station's helicopter, carrying a football with him to ease the jitters he felt from flying in the chopper. A few minutes later, it touched down in front of the state capitol building in Atlanta, a few blocks away from the stadium. Deion jumped into a car and was whisked to the ballpark. A security guard stopped the vehicle from entering a restricted area near the stadium. "We've got Deion in the car," one of the escorts shouted from the car window. Those magic words allowed passage, and at 4:38, Deion was inside, changing into his Braves uniform.

He was a pinch runner in both games of the doubleheader, stealing a base in the first one. Deion was available for nine of the Braves' last 12 games. Although he served mainly as a pinch runner and came to bat only once, his presence gave his team a psychological boost. The Braves won the National League Western Division title.

His teammates understood and appreciated the efforts he made to be with them. "Everybody loves him in our locker room, and the fans love him," said catcher Greg Olson. "I'm only surprised he didn't fly that helicopter in here himself and land it on the field."

The Braves beat the Pittsburgh Pirates in the National League Championship Series to advance to the 1991 World Series, which they narrowly lost to the Minnesota Twins. By this time, however, Deion had already returned to the Falcons.

With the help of a helicopter and a limousine, Deion made the trip from the football field to the baseball diamond to join the Atlanta Braves.

Missing the World Series was hard on Deion. "Killed me, 'cause it was the big game," he said. "I haven't been in a big championship game since Pop Warner."

The Falcons made the play-offs following the 1991 season, but Deion said it wasn't the same. "Wasn't the World Series," he said. "World Series is prime time."

"I've accomplished that other thing," he said, referring to his success in football. "Now it's time for me to accomplish a goal in this thing [baseball]: enormous success. I'm a good baseball player. I can be a star baseball player."

With Nixon still serving his drug suspension at the start of the 1992 season, Deion had the chance to play more often. He began drilling balls through gaps in the outfield and using his tremendous speed to run out triples.

He went on to his best year ever in baseball, hitting .304 in 97 games, stealing 26 bases, and leading the National League in triples. But when September came, Deion turned in his baseball spikes for football shoulder pads.

With the Braves in another pennant race, he again agreed to help them out down the stretch. This time, however, he went one better. He received permission from the Falcons to be with the Braves full-time during the league championship series and, if the team made it, the World Series.

The Braves assumed "full-time" meant he would give

Deion at bat during the 1992 World Series

up football completely as long as the Braves were alive in the postseason. During the league championship series against the Pittsburgh Pirates, however, Deion announced he still planned on playing with the Falcons in Miami on Sunday, October 11—even though the Braves were playing in Pittsburgh that same evening.

Deion returned punts and kickoffs, played cornerback, and even caught a pass on offense against the Miami Dolphins in the afternoon. With national media following him to record the event, Deion used helicopter shuttles and a chartered airplane to rejoin the Braves in Pittsburgh.

The Braves management was furious with Deion. They felt he had broken an agreement with them by playing with the Falcons that day. Braves manager Bobby Cox refused to put Deion into the game that night, even as a pinch hitter. As a result, Deion was denied the chance of actually playing in two professional sports in the same day.

The controversy died down a few days later when the Braves won the National League pennant. They were on their way back to the World Series. This time they would have their "Prime Time" player for the prime time event.

Few expected much of Deion. He had seen little action in the league championship series and did not play in the World Series opener against the Toronto Blue Jays.

But in game two, he started in left field. Determined to make the most of his opportunity, Deion reached base safely three times, scored a run, and stole two bases.

In game three, Deion came through with three more hits and another stolen base. Although Deion was doing well, the Braves lost both games in which he played. Even so, he was drawing praise from many people, including Braves general manager John Schuerholz. Schuerholz had been angry at Deion's decision to play football during the National League Championship Series. But by this time, even he had to admit, "You can see the excitement level of the club rise when he is in there."

Deion wasn't in the lineup in game four, which was won by the Blue Jays. The Blue Jays led three games to one and needed only one more win to capture the series.

Toronto had Jack Morris on the mound in the fifth game. At this point, the Braves were facing elimination. They had to score off Morris if they wanted to keep their championship hopes alive.

As Deion came up to bat, the game was tied 2-2 with two outs in the fifth inning and Otis Nixon on second base. Morris had used off-speed pitches to retire Deion on his first two trips to the plate.

This time, though, Morris delivered a fast ball. Deion lined it into center field to score Nixon with what proved to be the winning run. A few batters later, Deion himself scored when Lonnie Smith hit a grand slam home run to finish off Morris and break the game open.

Deion did his best to help the Braves again in the sixth game. He singled, doubled, scored a run, stole two bases, and even threw out a Blue Jay runner attempting to score. Despite these efforts, however, Atlanta came up short in extra innings and the World Series went to Toronto.

The Braves had lost, but Deion led both teams with a .533 Series batting average. He also had five stolen bases in the Series to tie with Nixon for the lead in that category.

Most of the Blue Jays and Braves players were off for a winter of rest. Deion, however, returned to work for the Atlanta Falcons.

A half circle and two short lines are drawn in the dirt with his bat—a ritual for Deion before batting.

Deion's dual sport accomplishments have brought him national media attention.

5
Highlight Films

NFL highlight films usually focus on the "glamour" positions of quarterback and running back. Deion, however, gets more than his share of time in the highlights. Fans are thrilled as he returns punts, kickoffs, and interceptions.

Deion broke into the National Football League with a splash, intercepting three passes in his first nine games and ranking among the leaders in punt returns in the National Football Conference (NFC). In his rookie season, he became the first Falcon ever to have his picture on the cover of *Sports Illustrated*.

People knew Deion was fast, but they were also amazed by his incredible acceleration. Most athletes have to run a few steps before reaching top speed. Deion appeared to be at full throttle from the very first step he took.

When he intercepted a pass, he was off and running

before anyone could touch him. In 1990, his second year in the league, he returned two interceptions for touchdowns. The following year, he had a spectacular runback after a lateral from teammate Tim McKyer, who had just intercepted a pass. "The guy took off so fast, I couldn't believe it," said his coach, Jerry Glanville.

Deion sometimes takes his turn on offense as well. In 1991 he was the only player in the league to intercept a pass, catch a pass on offense, return a punt, return a kickoff, and make tackles on both defense and special teams (punt and kickoff units).

With six interceptions that year, he tied for the NFC lead in that category (teammate McKyer also had six). In addition, he was twice named NFC Defensive Player of the Week, and he helped the Falcons make the play-offs for the first time in nine years. Then, in the first play-off game against New Orleans, he helped Atlanta to a 27-20 win by intercepting a pass in the end zone.

The Falcons' 1991 season finally ended with a loss to the Washington Redskins, who went on to win the Super Bowl. But Deion's season wasn't over. He started for the NFC and intercepted a pass in the Pro Bowl that was held the week after the Super Bowl. In addition to being named All-Pro, he was also recognized as Defensive Back of the Year by the NFL Alumni Association.

In 1992 the Falcons slipped to a 6-10 record and

missed the play-offs. But Deion continued to shine. He was voted the starting cornerback for the NFC in the Pro Bowl for the second year in a row.

Deion led the NFC in kickoff returns that year with an average 26.7 yards, and he returned two kickoffs all the way for touchdowns. He also played a bit of offense and even caught a pass for a touchdown.

The highlight films have recorded the versatile Deion finding his way into the end zone on kickoff, punt, and interception returns, as well as on a pass reception.

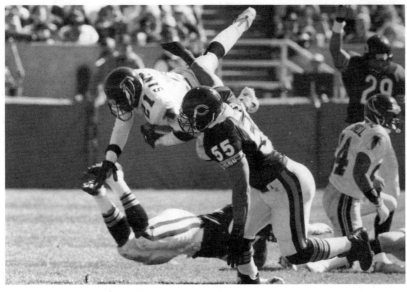

6
Prime Time

Many gold ornaments hang around Deion's neck, among them a cross and a dollar sign. More jewelry adorns his wrists, hands, and even one earlobe. His wardrobe includes more than 100 suits, 600 pairs of shoes, and countless hats and sunglasses. He thrills fans with marvelous moves as he snakes through defenders on his way to a touchdown. But those moves are nothing compared to the celebration dance he does when he finally reaches the end zone.

All are part of the Prime Time image of Deion Sanders. Although he acquired the nickname of Prime Time in high school, he didn't really develop the image until college. Before his final regular-season game for Florida State, he arrived at the stadium in a chauffeured limousine and dressed in a tuxedo.

The Prime Time image was carefully crafted to draw attention to Deion. Along with his performance as an athlete, the image helped him build a name for himself long before he reached the professional ranks. "I'm a businessman and my product is Deion Sanders," he once explained. "Prime Time is the way I market that product. I will do anything to promote that."

Deion has kept his flashy image confined to football. He's refused to sign as "Prime Time" when autographing baseballs. "I'm not Prime Time in baseball," he explained. "Only during football season. When I play football, I'm vocal, outgoing. In baseball, I'm more on the outside looking in."

Playing two sports has meant more than just a pair of paychecks. It has also made him very attractive to advertisers. Nike, the athletic shoe manufacturer, recognized the power of having Deion endorse their products and the company signed Deion to a million-dollar contract in 1991. The contract was only good, however, if Deion continued playing two sports.

While many assume Bo Jackson blazed the way for Deion, another football player—Jim McMahon—had a greater influence on him. McMahon quarterbacked the Chicago Bears to a Super Bowl championship in the mid-1980s and increased his fame, along with his income.

The connection between fame and income was not lost on Deion. "Jim McMahon is not, by far, the best quarterback in the NFL," Deion once said. But he quickly added that McMahon made huge sums of

Right: Nike pays Deion $1 million to endorse its products. Below: Deion credits former Chicago Bears quarterback Jim McMahon's image as well as his talent for McMahon's financial success.

money by endorsing products. "You think they pay Jim McMahon on all those commercials to be humble?"

But Deion turns the image off when he's out of the public eye. He prays before each meal and before going to bed. He doesn't drink alcohol and has never used drugs.

"If he's around a crowd of writers, he'll show off," said his college football coach, Bobby Bowden. "But by himself, he's very low-key and likeable, and a very kind person."

"It's like Michael Jackson," Deion says. "You think he wears that glove all the time? He puts it on for the show, then takes it off. That's how I am."

But on the field, Deion puts Prime Time to work and he has become a favorite of many fans. When he played for a Yankees minor-league team in Albany, New York, the organist played "On Broadway" when he came to bat. The scoreboard flashed the words, "What Time Is It?" The fans responded by yelling, "Prime Time!"

His style has also made him popular with his fellow players. A teammate on the minor-league team in Albany, Andy Stankiewicz, recalled the fun Deion could generate on bus trips. The players once held a mock trial and tried to fine Deion for dressing too nicely, wearing too much jewelry, and taking his cellular phone on road trips.

"Deion was pulling on his wallet and trying to buy

votes left and right," said Stankiewicz. "It was a riot."

Braves pitcher Steve Avery once commented about Deion, "The first thing I noticed was, the guy can talk. Boy, can he talk." Deion made fun of what he felt was Avery's lack of fashion sense. He turned fashion consultant for Avery, who admittedly dislikes shopping. Avery gave Deion $5,000 and told Deion to buy him some clothes. Deion had no trouble spending it all, plus another $1,000 he said Avery owed him. When Avery showed up wearing a flowered shirt and mustard-yellow pants, Deion said, "Now he looks like a man."

Deion's flashiness has drawn negative responses on occasion. Filmmaker Spike Lee criticized Deion's flamboyant style, saying Deion was not a positive role model for young people.

Not everyone agrees with Lee. William C. Rhoden, a columnist for the *New York Times*, wrote that Deion's "dogged pursuit of excellence and his self-styled formula for success: persistence, discipline, and sacrifice" are standards worthy of youngsters' admiration.

Rhoden added, "Too often sports role models preach conformity and order when the reality is that one must sometimes be different and a bit outrageous to achieve certain goals."

Deion believes that some of the criticism directed at him stems from the fact that he's African American. "On the field, I can't help getting excited about what

I do," Deion once explained. "In a white man, that's called confidence. In a black man, that's called cockiness, trash-talking."

Deion has had some minor run-ins with the law, which he also claims were caused by racial stereotypes. "If you're black and driving a [Mercedes] Benz and wearing a lot of jewelry, you're seen as a drug dealer," Deion explains.

Deion's efforts and his enthusiasm are appreciated by his team-mates.

But some people believe Deion is a troublemaker. In December 1988, during the week preceding his team's appearance in the Sugar Bowl, Deion was in a Fort Myers jewelry store. A dispute with a salesperson over whether Deion had paid for a pair of earrings turned into a physical confrontation. Deion ended up getting arrested and charged with simple battery and disorderly conduct. He was fined $800 and placed on probation for six months.

In May 1991, Deion was again arrested and charged with disorderly conduct. He reportedly cursed a police officer who had given him a warning for parking in a fire lane in Duluth, Georgia. Later that summer, as Deion was playing for the Atlanta Braves' minor-league team in Richmond, Virginia, he went into the stands to confront a couple of fans he said were harassing his girlfriend, Carolyn Chambers. Assault charges against him were dropped after he agreed to perform 100 hours of community service by coaching Little League baseball.

When he was with the New York Yankees in 1990, Deion received a brief lecture from Chicago White Sox catcher Carlton Fisk. Fisk criticized Deion for his failure to run after hitting a pop-up. "The days of slavery are over," Deion told Fisk. Fisk was angry that Deion implied he was a racist and the two exchanged words. Players from both dugouts charged onto the field, but order was quickly restored.

In October 1992, Deion became angry at television broadcaster Tim McCarver. McCarver said Deion had been "self-centered" for playing with the Atlanta Falcons at the same time the Braves were in the National League Championship Series. McCarver even suggested that Deion may have "gone back on his word" to the Braves. A few days later, the Braves won the National League pennant with an incredible ninth-inning rally in the final game of the series. McCarver was in the Braves clubhouse to interview some of the players as they celebrated their win. Deion got back at McCarver for his earlier criticism by dousing him three times with ice water. For his actions, Deion was fined $1,000 by the National League.

While many felt McCarver had gone too far with his comments, they also felt Deion was out of line. One person who came to Deion's defense was his girlfriend. "How can a person giving himself between two teams be self-centered?" asked Carolyn Chambers.

Deion likes to ignore the controversy and relax at home. Deion and Carolyn live in Alpharetta, Georgia, with their daughter, Deiondra, born in 1990.

"People don't see how tired he is when he gets home," says Carolyn. "He's so exhausted he doesn't want to eat. But he still doesn't neglect me or his daughter. He still gets up in the morning to take his daughter to school when he could be getting another two or three hours of sleep."

Even with two careers and a family, Deion still finds time for other activities. Fishing is one way he relaxes and, as one might expect, he has high praise for his own ability as a bass fisherman.

He can also unwind at home in his swimming pool, which is shaped like a football—complete with painted laces on the bottom. To give equal attention to his other sport, he has a round whirlpool spa with stitches painted on the bottom so that it looks like a baseball.

Deion is also a businessman. Besides his two full-time sports and his Nike endorsement contract, he is involved in several other ventures, including Deion's Hair Salon in Buckhead, Georgia. He also markets his own line of clothing, which bears a logo of a lightning bolt surrounded by the words "Prime Time."

Deion's life-style draws both positive and negative responses. But Deion never forgets the millions of young sports fans across the country who look up to him. "In the black neighborhoods, they've seen the dope man with all the chains," he says. "The kids love that stuff, looking nice with jewelry. I try to show them you don't have to be a dope dealer to get the jewelry. If I can do that in a positive image, I can help."

His goal is to open a youth center that will provide activities after school for kids and help keep them off the streets. "It would've been easy for me to sell drugs," says Deion. "But I had practice. My friends

Sharing a post-game celebration with his friend, rap star Hammer

who didn't have practice, they went straight to the streets and never left. That moment after school, that's the moment I want to grab."

Even while he works on the youth center, Deion helps his community in other ways. In 1991 he donated $10,000 to the United Way—the largest contribution made by any Atlanta athlete. The following year, along with his close friend, rap music star Hammer, he sponsored a basketball game between professional football and basketball players. The proceeds from the game were donated to the United Way.

Deion also has not forgotten the influence his mother had on him. "Whatever I needed as a child, she made sure I had. Now I want to make sure she has whatever she needs." He had a seven-bedroom mansion with an outdoor swimming pool built for his mother in Fort Myers. At the bottom of the pool, tiles spell out the words "Prime Time."

Deion's place in the spotlight continues. As he puts it, "People love me or hate me, but they always want to come out and see me."

Bob Hope poses with the 1988 All-America football team (Deion, No. 2, is in the front row).

Deion on defense for the Florida State Seminoles

58

DEION SANDERS
Florida State University statistics

FOOTBALL

YEAR	INTERCEPTIONS	PUNT RETURNS					BOWL GAME
		NO.	YARDS	AVG.	TOUCHDOWNS	LONGEST	
1985	1	30	255	8.5	1	58	Gator
1986	4	31	290	9.4	0	32	All-American
1987	4	32	381	11.9	1	53	Fiesta
1988	5	33	503	15.2	1	76	Sugar
Totals	**14**	**126**	**1,429**	**11.3**	**3**	**76**	

BASEBALL

YEAR	GAMES	AT-BATS	RUNS	HITS	AVG.	HOME RUNS	RBI	STOLEN BASES
1986	16	60	21	20	.333	1	14	11
1987	60	210	41	56	.267	3	21	27
Totals	**76**	**270**	**62**	**76**	**.281**	**4**	**35**	**38**

College World Series

YEAR	GAMES	AT-BATS	RUNS	HITS	AVG.	HOME RUNS	RBI	STOLEN BASES
1987	3	11	0	3	.273	0	0	1

National League statistics
New York Yankees, Atlanta Braves

YEAR	TEAM	GAMES	AT-BATS	RUNS	HITS	AVG.	HOME RUNS	RBI	STOLEN BASES
1989	Yankees	14	47	7	11	.234	2	7	1
1990	Yankees	57	133	24	21	.158	3	9	8
1991	Braves	54	110	16	21	.191	4	13	11
1992	Braves	97	303	54	92	.304	8	28	26
Totals		**222**	**593**	**101**	**145**	**.244**	**17**	**57**	**46**

National League Championship Series

YEAR	OPPONENT	GAMES	AT-BATS	RUNS	HITS	AVG.	HOME RUNS	RBI	STOLEN BASES
1992	Pittsburgh	4	5	0	0	0	0	0	0

World Series

YEAR	OPPONENT	GAMES	AT-BATS	RUNS	HITS	AVG.	HOME RUNS	RBI	STOLEN BASES
1992	Toronto	4	15	4	8	.533	0	1	5

NFL statistics
Atlanta Falcons

YEAR	GAMES	INTERCEPTIONS			
		NO.	YARDS	AVG.	TOUCHDOWNS
1989	15	5	52	10.4	0
1990	16	3	153	51.0	2
1991	15	6	119	19.8	1
1992	13	3	105	35.0	0
Totals	**59**	**17**	**429**	**25.2**	**3**

YEAR	PUNT RETURNS			
	NO.	YARDS	AVG.	TOUCHDOWNS
1989	28	307	11.0	1
1990	29	250	8.6	1
1991	21	170	8.1	0
1992	13	41	3.2	0
Totals	**91**	**768**	**8.4**	**2**

YEAR	KICK-OFF RETURNS			
	NO.	YARDS	AVG.	TOUCHDOWNS
1989	35	725	20.7	0
1990	39	851	21.8	0
1991	26	576	22.2	1
1992	40	1,067	26.7	2
Totals	**140**	**3,219**	**23.0**	**3**

Deion Sanders is the only player in Atlanta Falcon history to score touchdowns via punt, kick-off, and interception returns.

ABOUT THE AUTHOR

Stew Thornley is the author of several award-winning books on sports history. He has also written a biography for young readers, *Cal Ripken, Jr.: Oriole Ironman.*

A former sportscaster at radio stations in Missouri and central Minnesota, Thornley now resides in Minneapolis, a short distance from the diamond (above) on which he once served as batboy for the University of Minnesota Gophers.

ACKNOWLEDGMENTS

Photographs are reproduced through the courtesy of Jimmy Cribb, pp. 1, 9, 11, 35, 38, 40, 49 (top), 60, 62; AP/Wide World Photos, pp. 2, 28, 39, 44, 45 (both), 46, 58 (top); New York Yankees, p. 6; Kansas City Royals, p. 10; Dave Capel, pp. 12, 15, 17; Johnny Crawford, pp. 33, 56; Florida State University, pp. 18, 22, 24, 58 (bottom); Sam Lewis, Florida State University, p. 26; UPI/Bettmann, p. 43; Chicago Bears, p. 49 (bottom); SEBO, p. 52; Reuters/Bettmann, p. 64.

Front and back cover photographs courtesy of Jimmy Cribb.

Special thanks to Scott McClellan for his contribution of information.